# ALKALINE VEGAN FOR NEWBIES

## Easy 1-2-3 steps to quick alkaline vegan meals

By Nigel Robinson

I wrote this book because I wanted to live a healthy life. When I first ran across alkaline vegan groups and recipes I would start wondering where is the meat and what is used to replace the meat. I also find it hard to find the ingredients after I noticed all these people around me posting meals with ingredients I couldn't pronounce. So I set out to find ingredients on the list in my local supermarket that I could pronounce and relate to. There is a wealth of vegetables and spices that can be found in a local food store that doesn't require me to go through some middleman vendor for seasonings and ingredients. I watched others and studied various alkaline vegan recipes and came up with recipes that requires less than a quarter of the seasonings and ingredients on the approved alkaline vegan list. I hope you enjoy making these simple meals as I did. Much blessings and love from my plate to yours.

# Table of Content

# Approved Ingredients

| VEGETABLES | FRUITS | HERBAL TEAS | GRAINS | NUTS & SEEDS | OILS |
|---|---|---|---|---|---|
| Amaranth Greens - Callaloo | Apples | Allspice | Amaranth | Hempseed | Olive oil (do not cook) |
| Avocado | Bananas - Burro/mid-size (original banana) | Anise | Fonio | Raw sesame seeds | Coconut Oil (do not cook) |
| Bell peppers | Berries (no cranberries) | Burdock | Kamut | Raw sesame "tahini Butter" | Grape seed oil |
| Chayote | Cantaloupe | Chamomile | Quinoa | Walnuts | Sesame oil |
| Cucumber | Cherries | Elderberry | Rye | Brazilian nuts | Hempseed oil |
| Dandelion greens | Cherimoya – sugar apples | Fennel | Spelt | | Avocado oil |
| Garbanzo beans | Currants | Ginger | Teff | | |
| Green banana | Dates | Raspberry | Wild rice | | |
| Izote – cactus flower/actus leaf | Figs | Tila | | | |
| Kale | Grapes - seeded | | | | |
| Lettuce (all except iceberg) | Limes (key limes preferred with seed) | | | | |

| | | | | | |
|---|---|---|---|---|---|
| Mushrooms (all except shitake) | Mango | | | | |
| Nopales – Mexican cactus | Melons - seeded | | | | |
| Okra | Orange (Seville or sour preferred) | | | | |
| Olives | Papayas | | | | |
| Onions | Peaches | | | | |
| Poke salad | Pears | | | | |
| Sea vegetables (wakame/dulse/ arame/hijiki/nori) | Plums | | | | |
| Squash | Prickly pear (cactus fruit) | | | | |
| Tomato – cherry & plum only | Prunes | | | | |
| Tomatillo | Raisins - seeded | | | | |
| Turnip greens | Soft jelly coconuts | | | | |
| Zucchini | Soursops | | | | |
| Watercress | Tamarind | | | | |
| Purslane (verdolaga) | | | | | |
| | | | | | |

Juice of 1 key lime
2 apples
½ cup ice cubes
4 tbsp agave
4 cup coconut water
2-3 cups fresh strawberries

Combine all ingredients in a blender and blend until you get a smoothie like texture. Minus the ice and add a whole banana and you have a great breakfast meal. This one of the great things about alkaline vegan is you can blend practically anything together and get a great recipe. Don't be scared to try new things. Experiment and see what taste good to you and what doesn't. you can always switch out coconut water for spring water. I just love the taste of coconut water and how it makes me feel good after drinking it.

# Mango Juice

2 ripe mangos
Juice of 1 key lime
3 tbsp agave
3 cups coconut water

Peel the mangos and add to a blender along with the rest of the ingredients. These are very easy to make drinks. It is just the ingredients that is used to set them apart as alkaline. You can add ice or place inside your refrigerator for a few minutes to get a nice cold drink. Remember you can always substitute coconut water for spring water.

Soursop Juice

1 ripe soursop
3 tbsp agave
1 key lime
4 cups spring water

You can find this fruit in Caribbean grocery stores. It remains green when it is ripe, so when you buy it you can bring it home and until it is fit to be used. When it is ready for use you are going to need a big bowl. Peel the skin off the soursop. Remove all the seeds. Add the water and use your hands to mash and squeeze the soursop while in the water for about two minute. You can blend it if you want but remember to strain it through a cheesecloth when done. Sweeten the juice you squeeze from the cheesecloth and add ice or place in refrigerator until cool. You can use a strainer with small holes if you don't have a cheesecloth. In the island we would squeeze it through a clean t-shirt or fabric set aside just for that purpose. It can be quite pulpy hence the straining process.

2 large kale leaves
1 cucumber
4 cups spring water
4 tbsp agave

Combine all ingredients in a blender. Sweeten to taste. You can also add an apple to it if you would like. All drinks taste good to me when it is cold so if you would go ahead and add some ice or leave it to chill in your refrigerator.

$\frac{1}{2}$ cup blueberries
$\frac{1}{2}$ strawberries
4 tbsp agave
1 large kale leaf
4 cups spring water

combine all ingredients in a blender and blend until smooth. Add ice or chill in a refrigerator. Bon appetit.

1 banana
1 cup coconut milk
a pinch of sea salt
2 cups spelt flour
1 tsp sea moss
A pinch of all spice
$\frac{1}{2}$ tsp grapeseed oil

Combine all ingredients except grape seed oil in a mixing bowl. Heat your skillet to about 350 degrees Fahrenheit. Add the grapeseed oil then add your batter and cook your pancakes for about three minutes on each side. I would hope you have a nonstick skillet. Also it is best to heat the grapeseed oil for a minute before adding your batter. This way it helps to prevent the batter from sticking to the skillet. You can add spring water if you want to have thinner pancakes.

3 Green burro bananas
2½ cups of spring water
2 cups of coconut milk
1 tsp all spice
⅛ tsp sea salt
⅓ cup coconut milk

Wash and peel green bananas. You can do this by removing the tips of the bananas. Then slice the banana skin lengthwise. Break the skin off with your fingers in a circular motion around the banana. Similar to pegging an orange. Slice bananas into discs and puree in a blender. Add to a pot and boil for about 5 minutes. While it is boiling stir in the salt, coconut milk, and spice. I like to do most of my cooking on medium heat. I would turn up the stove on high, and once the food starts to boil I would turn it down to medium or level 4 and let it finish boiling.

# Fried Burro Bananas

2 green burro green bananas
2 tbsp of sea salt
3 cups grapeseed oil (or enough to cover bananas)

Remove the tips of the bananas. Slice banana skin lengthwise and peal with fingers all the way around. Slice bananas diagonal (slant) $\frac{3}{4}$ inch thick. Prepare a bowl with water and add the salt to the water. Then add the sliced bananas. Heat a skillet with grapeseed oil for deep frying. Stand back or prepare yourself for the oil to pop. Add the bananas from the bowl and let cook for 5 to 10 minutes turning them halfway through. Remove them and place them on a piece of paper towel. You can crush them with a plantain press or use the bottom of canned goods wrapped in aluminum foil. Place back in the salt water and then fry again for another 5 to 10 minutes.

1/4 cup Grapeseed Oil
1 tsp grounded papaya Seed
1 tsp Agave
1/4 tsp Sea Salt
2 tbsp Lime Juice
A pinch of basil
1 cup Mango (diced)
A pinch of onion powder

Blend all ingredients together for about 30 to 60 seconds.
Place in refrigerator for later use.

1 tsp Ginger (diced)
2 tbsp Sesame Seeds
1 tbsp Agave
2 plum tomatoes
1 tbsp Onion (diced)
1 tbsp Lime Juice

Blend all ingredients together. Place in refrigerator for later use.

2 tsp Agave
1 Cucumber (diced)
1 key lime
1/4 cup grapeseed oil
$\frac{1}{2}$ onion (diced)
1 tsp dill

Blend all ingredients together. Place in refrigerator for later use.

# Watercress Avocado Salad

A handful of watercress
½ avocado
A few raspberries

Wash raspberries and watercress and add to a plate with avocado. Add salad dressings from above for taste. Watercress have a strong taste to it. Just keep eating it while thinking of the great benefits of eating greens and get through your salad. It is mind over health over matter.

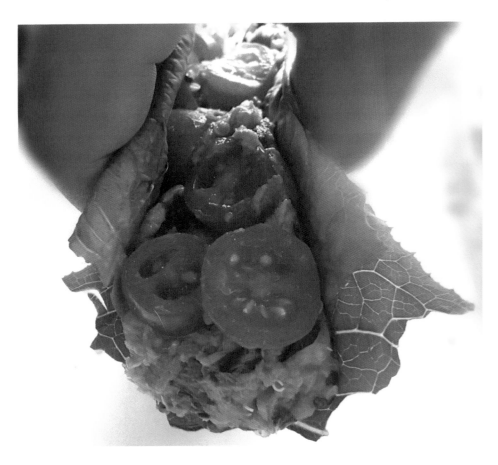

1 avocado
15 ounces of garbanzo beans
½ tsp sea salt
A few leaves of lettuce
Juice of 1 key lime
2 Oz. quinoa

cook quinoa separately or use raw if desired. Place all ingredients together except the lettuce leaves in a bowl. Use a fork to mash the ingredients in the bowl. Add ingredients from bowl to lettuce leaves.

Zucchini Squash Pasta

Small butternut squash (diced)
1 clove of shallot (minced)
$\frac{1}{4}$ tsp sea salt
2 large zucchinis
2 tbs olive oil

Prepare zucchini with a spiralizer or a julienne peeler. Peel and dice butternut squash $\frac{1}{4}$ inch thick. Add olive oil to a Sautee pan. Sautee butternut squash until golden brown or cooked. Then Sautee zucchini, sea salt and shallots with the butternut squash for about 2 minutes. You can garnish with more olive oil or any alkaline vegan oil of your choice.

# Butternut Squash Mushroom Dinner

1 butternut squash
1 tsp sea salt
1 tbsp olive oil
2 tbsp fresh basil
1 dozen plum tomatoes sliced in half
½ cup Minced onions
8 oz. of mushroom

Peel and boil butternut squash until fully cooked. Leave butternut squash separately and prepare the mushroom sauce. Add mushrooms, chopped onions, and plum tomatoes to a Sautee pan. Stir-fry until mushroom is slightly brown. You can add half a cup of spring water and mash some of the plum tomatoes in it. You can mash the plum tomatoes separately in a bowl, adding a pinch of spelt flour to thicken. Add contents of bowl to mushroom in Sautee pan and cook for about 3 to 5 minutes. I don't know why I have my salad in the same plate. I guess it's bad habit. You can make your salad separately.

# Mushroom Butternut Squash

By now you should be a pro at this. Prepare this meal using same ingredients. You can place your meal on top of a bed of kale on your plate. Sprinkle with key lime juice and enjoy. With most of these recipes you can add whatever from the list you are comfortable with. You can also garnish this with a few slices of avocado and make it your own recipe. You can also switch the rice for quinoa.

14 ounces of okra
1 dozen plum tomatoes (diced)
1 Small butternut squash (diced)
2 tbsp fresh basil (1 tbsp if dried)
1 tsp sea salt
1 whole onion (diced)
4 cups of spring water
1 tbsp olive oil

Combine ingredients in a pot and cook until squash is fully cooked. You can go ahead and crush the squash out inside the pot. If you want you can cook the squash separately, mash it with a fork. Add separately cooked squash after the other ingredients are cooked. Stir all ingredients together and allow to cook for another 3 to 5 minutes. You can add quinoa instead of squash. Season to taste.

# Garbanzo Bean Squash Soup

Using 14 ounces of garbanzo beans replaces the okra in the okra squash soup recipe. Most of the color comes from the squash and tomatoes. This is just to show different variations of making alkaline vegan soup by just switching out a few items.

Zucchini Mushroom Soup

1 -2 large zucchinis
8 oz. of mushroom
½ onion or whole shallot (diced)
4 cups spring water
1 tbsp olive oil
2 tbsp fresh basil (1 tbsp if dried)

prepare zucchini using spiralizer or julienne peeler. Add olive oil to a pot and stir-fry onions for about 1 minute. Add water and the rest of zucchini. Cook for 4-5 minutes or until vegetables are cooked. You can also add some chayote to cook along with the soup.

# Avocado Salad

This is not really hard to make. Dice some avocado with bell pepper of different colors, plum tomatoes, add some shredded lettuce. Sprinkle with olive oil or any alkaline salad dressing from above salad dressings. Minus the lettuce and avocado and you can stir-fry the vegetables along with some sliced onions. You can add this stir-fry to anything of your choice such as quinoa, squash or boiled burro bananas.

# Mash Potatoes (Burro Banana Style)

Bake or cook 2 green burro bananas. Mash them together in a bowl adding sea salt, basil, olive oil and approved seasonings. By now you should be pretty good at this. Just don't use too much salt. $\frac{1}{4}$ tsp of salt or a pinch should be good. I try to avoid using too much salt in anything I cook.

# Mashed Potatoes (Squash)

same directions as the mashed burro bananas recipe. Bake or boil squash then mash it together with a fork. Since virgin coconut oil is hard in cool temperatures, I add a little tablespoon on top like butter before serving it. There is organic hemp seed butter out there if you want to try that. Just check the ingredients before using it so you are still within the alkaline vegan guidelines.

TIPS

Sauce

You can make sauce to go with your meals by blending together in a blender plum tomatoes with peppers, onions, sea salt and grape seed oil. Don't use too much water as you don't want it to be thin. Use more plum tomatoes and onions if it is too thin. Store them in glass jars if you can. Glass jars like the ones below.

# HUMUS

Add to a blender half cup chickpeas, 2 small avocados, a teaspoon olive oil, a pinch of sea salt, juice of one key lime, a little tahini, a little bit of clove, approved peppers and blend to a puree. Garnish with a sprinkle of cloves.

## SPICES AND SEASONINGS

ACHIOTE ·
CAYENNE/ AFRICAN BIRD PEPPER ·
CORIANDER (CILANTRO) ·
ONION POWDER ·
HABANERO ·
SAGE ·

· BASIL
· BAY LEAF
· CLOVES
· DILL
· OREGANO
· PARSLEY
· SAVORY
· SWEET BASIL
· TARRAGON
· THYME

## THINGS TO SALT THE FOOD WITH

· PURE SEA SALT
· POWDERED GRANULATED SEAWEED
· (KELP/DULCE/NORI - HAS "SEA TASTE")

## APPROVED SWEETNERS

PURE AGAVE SYRUP - (FROM CACTUS) -
DATE SUGAR -

## BURRO BANANA

This banana is low in calories and provide very small amounts of fat. 8 amino acids your body cannot produce, potassium, fiber, vitamins B & C, calcium, iron, copper, selenium, phosphorous and magnesium are all provided by this fruit.

This is great for your heart because it replenishes the body's potassium levels.

Make sure you are you are eating fruits with seeds in them such as apple and seeded grape. This remove the possibilities that you are eating genetically modified foods.

## VEGAN SOAPS TO USE

If you have a baby or you would like to use vegan soaps, there are a few you can use. Dr. Bronner's unscented soaps and Shae Moisture carries vegan soaps that can be used on babies.

## HOMEMADE ALKALINE WATER

Squeeze 1 key lime in a gallon of water and let sit in your refrigerator overnight. You can just put the rest of the key lime in the water after squeezing the juice into the water before storing it away for the night. This will help make digestion better as it aide your liver in making more enzymes than your over-the-counter probiotics. Also the potassium in the lime interacts with the potassium in your body creating better electrical transmissions of your nervous system and your brain. Key lime fortify your heart with its magnesium content as well as protect your bones from rickets (vitamin D deficiency) with its calcium content.

# IRISH MOSS

Irish moss is loaded with trace minerals, iron, sulfur, vitamins, iodine, calcium, magnesium and selenium. It is a very energizing source of food that is very good for your skin and to keep your body in balance. Do not get the pale looking ones but instead the ones with a little browner color to it. Wash and soak about ½ ounce in warm water for 15 minutes. drain the water and add Irish moss and 2 cups of water to a blender. For an Irish moss ice-cream Add 1 cup hemp seed milk, ½ cup agave nectar, half cup grape seed oil or hemp seed oil and a pinch of salt. Blend together for a nice smooth sea moss ice cream. Place in refrigerator to solidify. You can add fruits such as strawberries and raspberries on top of the ice cream when ready to eat. It is a form of thickener so you can

Alkaline Vegan for Newbies

use it to thicken fluids, gravies, soups etc. you can also add it to your weight loss shakes. I bought mines on amazon looking for keywords such as "raw", "wildcrafted" or "wild harvested".

## DRINK YOUR WATER

Water is good for headaches, better mood, fatigue, boosting energy levels, constipation, getting toxins out of your body, digestion, weight loss, kidney stones, immune system, skin complexion, hangovers, back pain and to keep your body at the right temperature.

These are some of the herbs used by Dr. Sebi and are great medicinal herbs that can be used for teas as well as in pill form.

**Sarsaparilla Root Herb:**

The highest concentration of iron of any plant: Cures anemia, impotency in men, STDS, Herpes. Why is iron is so important? Iron is by far the most important in the mineral kingdom: Why? Because it's electrical; like the rest but it has magnet. It's the only magnetic nutrient in the ramification of life, because upon taking Iron, you take all the other minerals, proportionately balanced.

**Burdock Root Herb**

Burdock Root contains a number of medicinal properties that have been used for hundreds of years. Traditionally herbalists all over the world use burdock root as a blood purifier. It is the root of the burdock plant that is harvested for medicinal use. Burdock has been used by herbalists worldwide to treat a variety skin diseases such as abscesses, acne, carbuncles, psoriasis and eczema. Burdock can be either taken alone or combined with other remedies, such as yellow dock and sarsaparilla. The beneficial effects of this herb includes increasing circulation to the skin and helping to detoxify the epidermal tissues. Burdock Root has been reported to destroy bacteria and fungus cultures. It is a popular detoxifying agent that produces a diuretic effect on the body which aids the filtering of impurities from the bloodstream. By promoting perspiration, burdock root eliminates toxins through the skin by producing a detoxifying effect.

**Yellow Dock Root Herb**

Yellow dock root is a blood purifier and general detoxifier, especially for the liver. The herb, properly known as Rumex Crispus, supports detoxification from a few angles. First off, yellow dock root stimulates bile production which helps digestion, particularly of fats. Yellow dock root can stimulate a bowel movement to help remove lingering waste from your intestinal tract; it also increases the frequency of urination to assist in toxin elimination. Maintaining an efficient rate of waste elimination can help prevent toxins from accumulating in the liver, gallbladder and bloodstream, and helps circumvent the associated problems.

### Dandelion Herb

The health benefits of dandelion include relief from liver disorders, diabetes, urinary disorders, acne, jaundice, cancer and anemia. It also helps in maintaining bone health, skin care and is a benefit to weight loss programs. Bone Health: Dandelions are rich in calcium, which is essential for the growth and strength of bones, liver disorders. Dandelions can help the liver in many ways. While the antioxidants like vitamin C and Luteolin keep the liver functioning in optimal gear and protect it from aging, other compounds in dandelions help treat haemorrhaging in the liver.

### German Chamomile Herb

Calms the central nervous system and heals the brain. German chamomile is used for intestinal gas, travel sickness, stuffy noses, hay fever, nervous diarrhoea, attention deficit hyperactivity disorder (ADHD), fibromyalgia, restlessness, and trouble sleeping. It is also used for digestive system disorders, stomach ulcers, colic, and menstrual cramps.

### Elderberry Herb

For all coughs and flu or colds, and is considered my many to be the tastiest and most beautiful tea on earth! Elderberry is used for "the flu" (influenza), H1N1 "swine" flu, HIV/AIDS, and boosting the immune system. It is also used for sinus pain, back and leg pain (sciatica), nerve pain (neuralgia), and chronic fatigue syndrome. Some people use elderberry for hay fever (allergic rhinitis), cancer, as a laxative for constipation, to increase urine flow, and to cause sweating.

### Bladderwrack

Bladderwrack is a form of kelp that has been used medicinally for centuries. The main use of the herb has been for the stimulation of the thyroid gland as a treatment for obesity and cellulite. The high iodine content of the herb stimulates thyroid function which boosts metabolism. It has a reputation helping relieve the symptoms of rheumatism and rheumatoid arthritis and may be used both internally and as an external application for inflamed joints. Bladderwrack tea and bladderwrack powder are available to purchase.

**Organic Kelp/Seamoss Flakes**

One of the main benefits of kelp is its high content of iodine which is a mineral that is essential for the correct functioning of the thyroid gland. The thyroid gland regulates metabolism. If there is not enough iodine in the diet, the thyroid is forced to work harder than it should have to, eventually becoming enlarged. The tea removes the mucus from your body

**Irish Moss Seamoss Tea and Organic Powder**

Nutrition on a cellular level - nourish yourself back to health Irish Moss Powder - Nourish the cells, Sea Moss (also known as Irish Moss), as it turns out is nature's only plant based source of thyroid hormones, 92 minerals in each serving. It is truly one of nature's superfoods! Irish moss tea removes the mucus from your body,

**Bladderwrack Powder**

Bladderwrack powder is filled with minerals that help nourish and cleanse the skin of toxins that cause dryness, wrinkles and excess fluid retention, Because bladderwrack contains iodine, it provides a variety of benefits for thyroid health. As a thyroid stimulating property, bladderwrack may also regulate thyroid function and metabolism, Bladderwrack may also be used to help reduce inflammation and pain in joints caused by rheumatoid arthritis, in both internal and external forms of application and ingestion.

**Red Clover**

This herb is used to protect against cancer, to relieve/cure indigestion, high cholesterol, whooping cough, cough, asthma, bronchitis, and sexually transmitted diseases (STDs). Some women use red clover for symptoms of menopause such as hot flashes; for breast pain or tenderness (mastalgia); and for premenstrual syndrome (PMS). Red clover is applied to the skin for skin cancer, skin sores, burns, and chronic skin diseases including eczema and psoriasis.

### Red Raspberry

As its name suggests, raspberry leaf is the leaf of the raspberry plant. It is somewhat well known for its benefits during pregnancy, but it is beneficial to women at all stages of life. It is naturally high in magnesium, potassium, iron and b-vitamins which make it helpful for nausea, leg cramps, and improving sleep during pregnancy. The specific combination of nutrients in raspberry leaf makes it extremely beneficial for the female reproductive system: helping to eliminate/reduce fibroids. It strengthens the uterus and pelvic muscles which some midwives say leads to shorter and easier labours. It is good for overall uterine health.

### Stinging Nettle Leaf

In ancient Greek times, the stinging nettle leaf was used mainly as a diuretic and laxative. Now the plant is used for many cures. Illnesses it is used to help treat are cancer and diabetes. Nettle leaf is among the most valuable herbal remedies.

### Stinging Nettle Root

This is an astringent, diuretic, tonic, anodyne, pectoral, rubefacient, styptic, anthelmintic, nutritive, alterative, hemetic, anti-rheumatic, anti-allergenic, anti-lithic/lithotriptic, haemostatic, stimulant, decongestant, herpatic, febrifuge, kidney depurative/nephritic, galactagogue, hypoglycemic, expectorant, anti-spasmodic, and anti-histamine. Stinging nettle leaf and stinging nettle powder are now available on Dr Sebi's official site.

### Milk Thistle

The #1 recommended herb for liver health: the seed-like herb is so powerful and strong it is highly recommended for the treatment of liver disorders. These liver problems include cirrhosis, jaundice, hepatitis, and gallbladder problems. Milk Thistle actually grows new liver cells. Multiple studies suggest the benefits of oral milk thistle tea for cirrhosis. In studies up to five years long, milk thistle improved liver function and decreased the number of deaths in people with liver disease

## Cleavers

Herbalists have long regarded cleavers as a valuable lymphatic tonic and diuretic. The lymph system is the body's mechanism to wash tissues of toxins, passing them back into the bloodstream to be cleansed by the liver and kidneys. This cleansing action makes cleavers useful in treating conditions like psoriasis and arthritis, which benefit from purifying the blood. Cleavers is a reliable diuretic used to help clean gravel and urinary stones and to treat urinary infections. Cure your lymphatic system today!

## Allspice

This fragrant spice acts as a relaxant to aid stomach cramps and conversely acts as a stimulant to aid digestion.

## Black Walnut

Black walnut husks were shown to combat candida better than several commercial antifungal drugs. It is now found in many over the counter candida cures. It also kills parasites.Wild

## Cherry Herb

Along with coughs and colds, wild cherry bark is typically touted as a natural treatment for the following health problems:

• bronchitis

• diarrhea

• fever

• gout

• sore throat

• whooping cough

In addition, wild cherry bark is said to alleviate pain and stimulate the digestive system.

## Organic Kelp Granules

Strengthening of the circulatory system, provision of strong bones and teeth, cancer fighting benefits and reducing the risk of strokes and heart disease. The large concentration of iodine found in kelp helps to stimulate the thyroid gland and control metabolism.

## Blue Vervain

Calms the central nervous system. Vervain has been useful to herbal healers for many centuries of recorded history. Vervain's healing properties are attributed primarily to its bitter and stimulating effect on the liver and other organs, as well as its relaxing effect on the nervous system. Blue vervain is a herbal remedy that relieves respiratory and liver congestion, lower fevers, eases coughs and colds, cleanses toxins, calms the nerves and acts as a general tonic that produces an overall feeling of well-being.

## Shepherds Purse

Clean out your body! Shepherds Purse has detergent qualities: It is anti-diarrhoea, has antioxidant qualities and is anti-inflammatory and anti-mucus. Shepherd's purse heals. It is a urinary tract astringent and a uric acid diuretic. Dr Sebi speaks about this herb. Several studies indicate that shepherd's purse reduces mucus inflammation, protects against ulcers, and slows the growth of tumours. However, there is a lack of more recent research on shepherd's purse and its potential health benefits.

Shepherd's purse is typically used as a natural remedy for the following health problems:

•bladder infections

•bleeding disorders (including abnormally heavy periods)

•diarrhoea

•headache

•kidney disease

•low blood pressure

•menstrual cramps

•mild heart failure

• premenstrual syndrome

In addition, shepherd's purse is said to stimulate circulation and increase the flow of urine. When applied directly to the skin, it's used to promote healing from wounds and burns and to treat eczema.

**Yarrow Herb**

A super internal healing herb organ repair. Yarrow flower, used in chronic diseases of the urinary apparatus, is especially recommended as it exerts a tonic influence upon the venous system, as well as upon mucous membranes. It has been efficacious in healing sore throats, hemoptysis, haematuria and other forms of hemorrhage where the bleeding is small in amount, urinal incontinence, diabetes, hemorrhoids with bloody and mucous discharges, and dysentery. Also in amenorrhoea, flatulence and spasmodic diseases, and in the form of injection in leucorrhea with relaxed vaginal walls. It is found to be one of the best agents for the relief of uterine fibroids.

**Chickweed**

Chickweed tea is helpful as an aid in weight loss. It is well known among the herbalists that chickweed suppresses appetite. Chickweed is said to soothe hunger pangs as well as minor irritations in the digestive tract. When chickweed is combined with other herbs that also help with appetite suppression it becomes a super herb. As a diuretic it helps flush your system of excess water by increasing the amount of urine you secrete. a demulcent (forms a soothing film over a mucous membrane, relieving minor pain and inflammation of the membrane).

**Black Cumin Seeds**

Black Cumin seeds, also known as Nigella Sativa, has been used to successfully keep people super healthy for over 3,300 years, since their first reported discovery in Egyptian Pharaoh Tutankhamen's tomb. Part of the buttercup family, the seeds are dark, thin, and crescent-shaped when whole. There have been reports of these "health giving" seeds used throughout history in the Middle East, the Mediterranean and India, from minor headaches and skin irritations to otherwise deemed "impossible circumstances." Regarded throughout the entire Middle East as one of the most powerful anti-inflammatory herbs ever to exist...

*Cleopatra used it as a beauty treatment.

*Queen Nefertiti used black seed oil to bring luster to her hair and nails.

*Hippocrates used it to assist with digestive and metabolic disorders.

*Archaeologists even confirmed King Tut kept a bottle of black cumin Seed Oil in his tomb – for use in the afterlife.

**Stinging Nettle Root Powder**

For smoothies it is used for many conditions. Stinging nettle root is used for urination problems related to an enlarged prostate (benign prostatic hyperplasia [BPH]). These problems include night-time urination, too frequent urination, painful urination, inability to urinate, and irritable bladder sydrome (IBS). Stinging nettle root in powder form is also used for joint ailments, as a diuretic, and as an astringent for urinary tract infections (UTI), urinary tract inflammation, and kidney stones (nephrolithiasis). It is also used for allergies, hay fever, and osteoarthritis. Use stinging nettle for internal bleeding, including uterine bleeding, nosebleeds, and bowel bleeding. Other uses include anaemia, poor circulation, an enlarged spleen, diabetes and other endocrine disorders, stomach acid, diarrhoea, dysentery, asthma, lung congestion, rash and eczema, cancer, preventing the signs of aging, "blood purification," wound healing, and as a general tonic.

**Dandelion Powder**

Dandelion Powder is used for loss of appetite, upset stomach, intestinal gas, gallstones, joint pain, muscle aches, eczema, and bruises. Dandelion powder is also used to increase urine production and as a laxative to increase bowel movements. It is also used as skin toner, blood tonic, and as a digestive tonic. Use it to treat infection, especially viral infections, and cancer. In foods, dandelion is used as salad greens, and in soups, wine, and teas. The roasted root is used as a coffee substitute. Dandelion contains natural alkaline chemicals that increase urine production and decrease swelling (inflammation).

**Black Walnut Hulls Powder**

Benefits of Organic Black Walnut Hull:-

•Supports healthy digestion and bowel regularity

•Provides oxygen to the blood

•Helps balance blood sugar

•Powerful detoxifier

Harmful organism cleansing with black walnut hull in powder form produces a potent elixir that is toxic to harmful organisms.

**Valerian Root herb**

Valerian is most commonly used for sleep disorders, especially the inability to sleep (insomnia). It is frequently combined with blue vervain, german chamomile, or other herbs that also cause drowsiness. Valerian is also used for conditions connected to anxiety and psychological stress including nervous asthma, hysterical states, excitability, fear of illness (hypochondria), headaches, migraine, and stomach upsets. Some people use valerian for depression, mild tremours, epilepsy, attention deficit hyperactivity disorder (ADHD), and chronic fatigue syndrome (CFS). Valerian is used for muscle and joint pain. Some women use valerian for menstrual cramps and symptoms associated with menopause, including hot flashes and anxiety.

**Anamu** kills cancer cells - Laboratory investigations show that anamu retards the growth of several strains of cancer and leukemia cells. In a plant screening programme performed at the University of Illinois at Chicago, more than 1,400 plant extracts were evaluated for the prevention and treatment of cancer. Anamu was one of only 34 plants identified with active properties specifically against cancer.How does anamu work against cancer?Several phytochemicals in anamu like astilbin and dibenzyl trisulphide have been documented to directly kill cancer cells. Research showed further that the compounds in anamu were able to differentiate between normal cells and cancer cells, killing only the cancerous cells. In addition, other substances in the herb stimulate the body's natural defences as described below.Anamu stimulates the immune system - Anamu has also been verified to have immunostimulant properties. It stimulates the immune system to increase its production of lymphocytes and natural killer cells - powerful disease-destroying cells. At the same time, it increases the production of interferon and interleukins - substances naturally produced by the immune system in fighting cancers and infections.Anamu fights infections - It demonstrates broad spectrum antimicrobial properties against numerous bacteria, viruses, fungi and yeast. Compounds in anamu directly kill and or inhibits the growth of these germs. Interestingly, many alternative medicine practitioners believe that infection plays a major role in many cancers. Anamu is widely used in folk medicine for treating infections.Anamu relieves pain - Its traditional use as a remedy for arthritis and rheumatism has been validated by clinical research that confirms its pain relieving and anti-inflammatory effect. Researchers in Sweden demonstrated its COX-1 inhibitory properties (cyclooxogenase-1 inhibitors are a new class of popular and profitable arthritis drugs). Anamu extracts have been found to relieve pain and inflammation even when applied topically to the skin.Anamu lowers blood sugar - While anamu has not been widely researched for diabetes, it had been documented to lower blood sugar levels by more than 60 per cent in laboratory animals. This reflects herbal medical practice in Cuba where anamu has been used as an aid for diabetes for many years.

Alkaline Vegan for Newbies

*Anamu has been found to cause contractions of the uterus that can lead to abortions and miscarriages. As such, it should not be used by pregnant women.*Anamu contains a low concentration of a blood thinner called coumadin. People with any bleeding disorder like hemophilia or who are on blood thinning medication should consult their health-care provider before using anamu.Directions for useI recommend using organically grown anamu herb, free of insecticides, herbicides and other pollution.One heaping tablespoonful of the whole powdered anamu plant is diffused in one litre of hot water. The resulting tea is drunk preferably on an empty stomach. An average dosage is four ounces (about half a cup) twice daily.

**Lilly of the Valley**: Lily-of-the-valley is a plant. The root, underground stem (rhizome), and dried flower tips are used to make medicine.

Lily-of-the-valley is used for heart problems including heart failure and irregular heartbeat. It is also used for urinary track infections (UTI's), kidney stones, weak contractions in labor, epilepsy fluid retention (edema), strokes and resulting paralysis, eye infections (conjunctivitis), and leprosy.

Store lily-of-the-valley in well-sealed containers and protect from light.

PLEASE DO NOT USE ANY INGREDIENTS YOU ARE ALLERGIC TO. IF YOU ARE NOT SURE CHECK WITH YOUR DOCTOR FIRST. THANK YOU.

Thanks for buying my book and I hope it helped you a lot. A few tips to remember is to cook most of your meals on medium heat. You can add ginger to almost everything except the ones with any vegetable or nut milks added. Ginger goes well with most of the drinks as well except soursop or any drink that use vegan milk. Always understand that when wet ingredients are added to hot oil there will be popping of the

**Alkaline Vegan for Newbies**

oil that can flash out of the pot and burn you. Cook with responsible. Best of luck.

Printed in Great Britain
by Amazon